The Hard Return

The Hard Return
Marcus McCann

INSOMNIAC PRESS

Library and Archives Canada Cataloguing in Publication

McCann, Marcus, 1983-
The hard return / Marcus McCann.

Poems.
ISBN 978-1-55483-063-3
Ebook ISBN 978-1-55483-076-3

I. Title.

PS8625.C365H37 2012   C811'.6   C2012-900769-2

The publisher gratefully acknowledges the support of
the Canada Council, the Ontario Arts Council,
and the Department of Canadian Heritage through the
Canada Book Fund.

Printed and bound in Canada

Insomniac Press
520 Princess Avenue, London, Ontario, Canada, N6B 2B8
www.insomniacpress.com

THE CANADA COUNCIL | LE CONSEIL DES ARTS
FOR THE ARTS | DU CANADA
SINCE 1957 | DEPUIS 1957

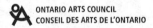

ONTARIO ARTS COUNCIL
CONSEIL DES ARTS DE L'ONTARIO

Contents

So we became transformed, and refused to believe we'd ever be destroyed because we were not only ourselves but everyone and everything.

— David W. McFadden

Prayer
To be read aloud in unison

Non-proprietary methods of composition:
collaboration, enmeshment, mutually assured
instruction, Hail Mary, heightened sense of self.
Shoulder to shoulder, odd phalanx of bowled-over
lover-friend-lovers. Cosmic spirals of communication,
retuning, junk talk, yammer, here is a voice
and we are using it.

Here is a voice and we are using it.
Loose, jangly, not-quite-unison,
discording. Us in a nighttime parking lot,
song-spilled, gin-singed, stab-slatted, yonder-longing
sketching on the side of a convenience store
that we are rattled. We use our hand sparingly.

Rickety wicker of our common selves.
Brittle, inhibited, possessive, jealousy ours,
especially. Us or a common alternative supplied.
Our shares in publicly traded company
indeterminate and valuable. Pleasingly left
guessing in the futures market.

At First I Felt Small, and Then

I felt big.

I felt teen hormones,

like gas
getting heated,

like — on Adelaide Street — a gang
of dancerats on the sidewalk, lolling.

Like a hole in the ground
growing a condo;

like the achievable Internet,
like my chat log,

like an explanation
put off but brewing.

I felt like my debts.

I felt like an endless game of
You're awesome. No, you're awesome.

Danger Overhead

Scaffold like a verandah, plywood

thought bubble, empty, empty. A plank thorax
on metal legs, a cage after escape, a wobbling

stripper set. Labourers assembled it in winter.
I admit, it went over my head. As for the workers,
it's the actual law and not its letter
they followed, thank god. At night, walkers —

black-jacketed, with hair the wind ransacks,
singing tiny duets with their thoughts, warbling

emails, lists, not one exactly "pedestrian" —
are momentarily aware of and protected
from the danger overhead. So says the sign.
Or the sign says the opposite. *I've warned you, kid.*

Now you're on your own. I can't tell, but maybe you could.

Pipe

A thumb-sized membrane, veined, a glass organ
streaked like sugar cane, fading flashlight, art lab —
brown bits of brain stem blown through a straw onto acetate.

A groove for all tongues — prissy, jagged —
where to whisper, to applaud the wind
our fleshy self hauls on fire, atmosphere, chemical admission.

Its narrow corridor: embroidery floss, bullet train,
urgent dandelion stem, urethra.

What little we know about want: that it singes fingers,
that it can fill a lung with paste.
That you can be both pickled with it and raw.

Machine, oh medical device, oh vehicle with all-wheel drive,
counterweight in the hand, light as a paper penny tube.

Earthenware Mug

Never forget, dear reader, that you hate the morning.
— J. Thomas Robinson

Part mustang, part gumboot. Part Reichstag,
part umbrella: truck tire wheel well
of the morning. Chunky hollow potato
you float your musings over, arms
pinched to your body, tucking its brunt
under your gloomy pit. The uneasy gumbo
of your morning thoughts
percolated, filtered and a little
sweetened. Winds that blew fall blow
winter now; heavy twist and giving up of snow

like a knotted bundle of patch cords
in the ganglia, piping regret in on loudspeakers.
A cup is an amplifier, a mug's genius
is it's never used that way.
Instead, its tug like Graham's
dinner parties, a gravy tureen, dish
after dish of steamed legumes — wet heats
lapping at your neck, vacant and grinning.
Morning's roll call makes you squeamish,
it slump-hulks in from west of the river out of a greenish

twilight like dark jelly.
You're already solving the to-do list's
sudoku, a fill-in-the-blank barracuda

circling, circling, its metal fins clang, ring
in the disordered forest of your porch:
cash in lieu, day in lieu, the
grimy musicking of the main drag
chiming in. You lay it at the feet
of bad weather: atmosphere brewed a
balls-kicked cloud, then sleepwalks down the valley through the

town, slipping past the seams of insulation
and into your chest. Never mind. There are choices
to make, two types of breads
in the fridge, there's Cheerios or Life.
Attach an emotional peg leg
or use a crutch. Take your meds
or be sad all the time, you think
while showering, everyone in the city showering,
water running down their backs like lug treads,
muscle of four thousand cranes, the light of their red foreheads.

Puffy Coat with a Hole Burnt into It, Bringham Street

A polyester coat is no shortcut to happiness.
Just ask this one, its sheath split, its stuffing finally
offering that extra pocket you wanted.

A coat that learned the line between keeping warm
and on fire is like the metal skeleton inside a trampoline,
a hoop of safety that is, incidentally, dangerous.

Is this a too-poorly fireproofed coat or all-too-fireproof
    kindling? —
now brûlée, coarse black salt ringing something tequilic,

new blackragged zipper teeth looking for their other half
to kiss — those who dare to wonder, wonder.

Tee

In the closet, a Warhol wanting
a hug. A flag. A loaf in a drawer —
blank-faced, a gift receipt —

its fabric hinges
creased, the crease a settlers' museum
you can follow with your finger.

Everything warps, even your running tee;
after wearing it, how it surrenders
its shape for you.

How it smells like you, only worse.
How it flattens itself against the floor,

wallflower — floor flower. It loves, and

therefore is sad, like us. But,
when pulverized, it grows softer,

so unlike our other friends,
so unlike them.

Dunk Tank

The marine glory of *gotcha*, and *gotcha back*. Chloronic
holding pen of those we schmucked. Hocking a loogie kicked
up a notch — systemic — made ungainly, the mass

of a full-sized four-door beater. Gallons and gallons of *the
    colder*
the better suspended between clear Perspex, the safest
glasslike plastic on the planet, its hind square painted

radiant college-slut blue. The seat — like a fin, a skateboard
deck made hinged, spindly — cupping the bum of a gym
teacher in a swimsuit. Not the coquette, the run and hide,
    the hermit —

thrush in the pool's mouth kisses his feet.
A game of social studies, three balls for a dollar, three
chances to overturn the static, the goading, drop a bully

like a bully drops a bran muffin, chances that depend
on how eager the arm is to catch the light, how rigged it is.
Equitable estoppels, a ratio of vex to velocity, *you've made
    your bed,*

now swim in it cut with *it's all for a good cause.*
And after, they'll empty, collapse; it's rented,
so whatever was in us that's gleeful, a truck hauls off at four.

Scene in Which a Neighbour Tries to Jump from Your Window onto His Own Roof

Dropped like a typo, like an amped epaulette, a stiletto,
foot psalm in a placebo of place, mid-air,
in a thickest-chicken-bone popped-cartilage pose,

he a taut package of surface on tension, pent-up,

the neighbour's sloped shingled roof teasingly near,
his leg a finger caressing its eaves —

below, fence slats sulk, threatening to kick the disks in
    his back askew.

Watch. The clanging glamour of approach he commits to
jokes *oopsie, pookie*. As the Ponzi hangs — a spill of
    pilsner, grappa —

you want to seam-ripper the idea, try needlepoint,
    appliqué.

He's suspended a porno of oppositions,

his particles part, the pause's bowed drywall takes bets
on the boxing match of spent jerk vs. Zappa plunge.

And caught in pestle and grist, hassle and pest,

you — wimp, worrywart, Pythagorean pilot of plan B,
oh, you bookish pansy — wait for the unclenching whup,

for his frame to tap the coup he's singing.

Beerdancehallmusic

Foyer salted the street, the city sideways. Night claps.
What's electric charges down the sidewalk, the rest
cartwheels behind, wind-resistant, a parachute on legs.
Residential turns mixed, turns into commercials.

Our leash slacks,
an instant teller logics out cash, briefly psychic.
Money is brighter and less important then —
excuse me — *than* booze. Then booze:

change piles up, we toggle ten links of a hoist chain
to our soft inside pocket, dance like we got hooked on
croquet and No-Doz. Mucking about
in our rucksack skull, cells spin like compass needles.

A stocky scrum slow-mos over, gets handsy.
Skunky buds pair up, some strip to their trunks. Overcome,
we slip into their crooks. We sweat gobbledygook. Ex's big
trap door gives and they decamp. No matter.

We collapse like a lung, the bar exhales us.
We wanted syntactics and got it, then didn't know what.
We split into tag team cab teams, skins
punt. Later, we say the night never clapped.

Hassle Free Clinic, Toronto

My torso a rabbit ear above him.
Waistband at my knees, knees like feet

I use to stand on shins.
The inkjet in my head spits reams.

Being always-forever-constantly
my mind's elevator music, sex —

if I had to, I'd say *a half cup of sugar poured
into a shot glass.* Or I'd say,

*I want to knock down a wall in my chest
and make room for more furniture.*

With a cotton swab, the doctor
asks if some encounter is still riding my blood

ready to lick its thousand lips and work
the humble spell of photosynthesis in my tracts,

to bloom and overfill in someone else.

Song for the Song of Britney Spears

Lullaby sung through a microchip kazoo. Charged warble.
A woman with a metal mouth, a blinking light in her voice
saying, *excuse me, sir, if I might have one word....*
Under "artist": file as "cyborg."
White woof of the scrambled, the unattached, the loose,
the lost. Pulse of the dazed
sonic pheromone of the halved heart.
That no producer can scrub

from the bend in her voice
its high lonely drone speaks to our ears' empathy.
Britney a radiator. Shock absorber.
Story of the holy fool told in escalating burps,
it pipes into a public-private place —
the lost pulse of the dazed
sonic pheromone of the halved heart
that no producer can scrub —

and every antennaed body, every upright metal,
everything in sight that skitters and twitches mouths the
       words.

Poem for a Precious Chapbook

A bird with a bum wing, it limps
like limping had valour. Pigeon-

coloured crook puts air in a headlock,
waits for air to pass out.

Wrench of the racketeer, the revolutionary —

you haven't been this scared of paper
since Valentine's Day. Pilates of the page
holds an opposing position — a puppet

echoing its author: talk, talk, talk,
then applauding itself. And always inserting

nonsense, it mimes: caret, less than, L, V,
greater than, seven and, in French, *accent circumflex*.

Poem for a Precious Chapbook

If spine is sheep, a fold
is a fold.

If spine is a wallet, fold
is a billfold.

If spine is *gimme one good reason*, fold
is twofold.

If spine is a puzzle, fold
is baffled.

If spine is smothering grandma with a pillow, fold
is her, muffled.

If spine is a whip and harness, fold
is a blindfold.

Twenty-Two Toronto Poets Wake up on the Bathroom Floor and Discuss Their Hangover

It is spring over the porcelain bowl
and needs total silence. It carries you

hacking the day into shape on the phone, there is still no
water and erotics
to show I was prepared to die. Here, orange
stares at the grief-plunge.

I call myself every bad word I know.

That round of steamed, shaped, rehardened wood
wanted to be looked at. I know now what I missed.

Self flagellation working up to a congratulation
written: and glances. Orange
has blown his brains out, we go our separate ways.

It is, being human, to have won from space
spaces and if this were a boat
I'd thought there would be more of us. Considering

the hug-and-petters that can not or won't quit:
Wham! Nothing, abortion, leukemia.

And I will neither soak my brain in brine
or what the wallpaper is concealing.

Eyebrows learn to speak.
I made the spearheads thin
and gristle-smiled.

A Flip-Flop

Enact the strap of a toy purse. Carry a shoe.
Appear edible. Toggle a long tongue,
make our feet gossip. Ribbon licorice,
a bridge standing on its hands,

stencil, packing foam, pool toy:
outdoorsy marshmallow not too far off
the paved lot of our exploits,
like a peach by October turned to stone,

the frost by which it's changed to wood:
a boxed-up cottage, slowing into prose.
Brace bracket of tan, henna tattoo of childhood,
it's not time to come in, no, never time to come in.

Co-worker's House Party

Wading through the plush carpet of obligation,
a tinted cellophane soirée that brings out goodwill's
    gold-painted platter
from the upper cupboards of our public relations
    repertoire —

we carpoolers, starry from smudging the highway
like a thumb across fluorescent cake crumbs, succumbed
    for a bit.

Carol's white-lacquered bell caused baked goods to get
    swapped. We split up.
Schoolboys of politeness, we talked like a reverend
was in the room, rapt mimicry of chatter by the spouses'
    baseline
for a mashup of rehashings and gossip lite.

God, was it eggnog that made our judgement gauzy?

We snuck onto the porch to blaze. Inside, we lingered in
    the house's back forty,
found a cup of chocolate-covered coffee beans, their
    glittery waxes
like motor oil, shellac, black chess pieces from a plastic
    set,

and turning over each marble, we faced them like the

end of a telescope,
a tiny camera lens recording our tics.

Rower

Angular jag of gym equipment, a failed
experiment plotted on a graph — one, one, one,

one and a half — or

who was watching stopped
too soon, the shebang slightly out of the

data set — a breakdancer doing the Spy Crouch

a split second before he flips his body
onto its fingertips.

Maybe. But read the other way, this lug tends

to zero, a stainless stretch, practice-lobbing
bricks from the church of Everything Is Illusion —

curt, tensile — going nowhere —
even less than that, I guess, if it weren't for

its ripcord, a chain dowel of bark so high-strung
it flexes its chassis, wrought ribbon

a zipper of depth charges, a stamen
auditioning for a horror film, like Epstein

would sculpt it, eulogizing bulk as inhale.

Dawn Lightning, Reflected in a Glass Condo

The world is not exactly where you left it.
Ecstatic, frazzled, stuttering, a tower

bounces on its soles, a fourth-grader
playing dodgeball. Its parallel lines

hiccup. With enough light,
everything comes unsewn.

The break is the *break* inside
nervous breakdown. Then,

dark pulls the plug, settles in
like a former classmate settles into

stalking you on Facebook. It is calm,
but there is no reason to feel safe.

That there is no reason to feel safe
is highlighted by a new vein of white

fudge crackle sliding across
the building's glass front, saying,

No. Keep your guard up,
and, *the ball's in your court.*

What causes what is unclear,
but the sky heats up at the sides,

electric edifice ceding
to its analog environ. A low ceiling of clouds

swells with black light. The hour
hums like a brother interrupting

bullying. You expect
and are surprised by the morning.

The tower isn't ready to dry its eyes,
not yet. But don't worry. It will.

Compiling, Collated

A humid boutique of handmade bath salt, legs-split joy,
brine for the eye, lying like vinyl chairs, choke-clutched, rival:

shirts shed like a redacted chiffon tress of static at our
    knees —
James like white plastic, Dracular, shiny — his navel a hard
    return

from his surly-nerved poem-scraped cock: me charmed, focal,
one stray thought from comic. Cocks like kazoos. Cocks like
    fajitas.

Like wet remotes. Us mucus. Us sinew. Lockjawed. Track-
    hewed.
Membrane of our toggling bauble caught mid-spike, we pause,

document — lock in — dark serifed hairs on titanium white,
rosé. Archival. A kiss of electric fields, nearness, affinity, a gift
    to wait for.

Shoulder to shoulder, a tiny squadron, sweaty company's
    smallest —
a two-person — department. Then blurring, pixilated, turning

to goop; then like melted soft serve, milky, watery, separating.

Pale Anonymous Hetero, Havoc Comes

I'll be he, Mr. Member Renew, renew me.
Member renew. I'd Sly Tom him in
a washtub, in a hot chop testament to largess. Pale
anonymous hetero, havoc comes. I ache, I even spun

thunder. Oh we wet youth, aura, erections
woof. Cause a hit. Youth,
nude ace, abstinent twink who'd bug us to, I
jet mucus, woken hot

to camera them, daze sky (x3).
Boy's lips.

Hothead pant, you earthmen, I hit a ____. I love our effigy.
Twitch tube ink, itchy lava, doesn't my
condom, yawn, uhh, woo you? You'd woo you, eh? Oh woo
    woody, intrude, hook you.
Orally yo-yo, orally blush. He's Internet hunky. Raucous
    yahoo CIA:

we'll daze them camera to sky (x3).
Use milk jet.

Twenty-Two BC Poets Use Orgasm As a Metaphor for Belonging

Come my ivory gal, ride up on my charger —
when he fingers his nipples
thumb on the wet drapery
my crevices all hot for him

that warmth in my mouth:
a meditation
thrusting its paper body up from the fist
into and out of mean limbs of the rattled

growing, eating themselves
partner to partner until you discover
transformation, so by dawn, I'd be raw
& dying on the field. It is a playing field

curling behind her ears
or his slender legs, like a girl's, kicking under him?

My back was heavy, drenched with space
on the supple sufficiency of her body.

Its bum left to bob like a yoo-hoo to a tummy
its snowy fur. Not the mechanical slide

directly into the auditory nerve
under her vocabulary. Later

nothing prepares you
to touch down a few inches from where you stand.

Medical Devices

In the cupping care of their moulding,
they are all the same. Their seam-sanded sides.
Their rounded edges, empathic. Willing to.

Feedback on the wet face of an animal familiar.
Clever, even-tempered.

Yes, so even as to appear
unmoved. But not, their quiet fingers

in your throat, or
                        hugging your artery, or
just holding your arm, squeezing —

anyway, it's not what they do,
it's how they, ashen, stand

each a half pace off, like a girl
you're slowly falling out of love with,
more and more — though trying not to be — in your way.

Chicken Wings

Meat crabapples. Meat mangoes.
Viscous meat cherry bombs
held together by the oxblood of pubs.

And to be foodlike, a David Cronenberg set piece,
meat of our parties, our rowdiness,
meat of our one-too-many pints
and maybe-I'll-take-the-back-roads-home,
plans both B and C.

And unlike its cousins, the finger
and burger, its bones

are revealed, inert, at the end of the show.

Oversized Gold Lamé Handbag

A purse that relies on its stitching
the way a drag queen relies on eyelashes.
A purse that sucks in her stomach.
A purse that says *to die for*,
meaning *to die with style*. Or even *to die of style*.
A purse that works our desire
for magic, which starts as sun-kissed tinsel
and hides supplies.

Straight Pins

Around an acetate campfire, backed by card: sixty
for a dollar. Dummy pins, placeholder pins,
where a sewing needle's eye is

is an Easter pearl like a cloudy pupil:
chick yellow, enamel pink. Dim purple.
Hold that fold — you cannot sew a seam
without straight pins.

Or, you can. A needle is a rock
star, straight pins bald, half-deaf techies.

A man staging a football
for a punt kick. Handrail. Rail tie.
TV Guide. Wingman. Audio tour of the museum,
its foam on your ear. They all look the same.
You cannot tell them apart, pause, em dash.

Garbage Chute

Reader, do you remember filing cabinets?
Their cool bodies aloof, secretarial. Like that,

but in our common hall, water
closet for our food scraps, wrappings.

Snake throat with fifty steel faces
measuring trash by its circumference.

Want its heart to sing? Drop a box of screws,
a wine bottle. Hold its lower lip a minute.

Num, num, num. Throat gurgle. *Clang.*

And when, soon, this tower teeters, glass gone,
rebar overgrown, its spine

arthritic, the chute will not say
I told you so. It will not say anything.

Scaffolds, Dismantled

Where their metal hooves all winter stood:
they sweat rust into concrete. They stain

what they meant to protect. The wood
planks too greyed in winter, the lane

now stacked with them. Scaffold like a hood
popped, I can see what arcane

secrets the building holds. Not much. Good.
More secrets in the scaffold, a rickety biplane

reverse-engineered on the lawn, a skid
of giant prayer cards for the weather-beaten,

the discoloured,
the shrunken,

juice leaching into sidewalk and sod,
leaving, around what lasts, at last, an outline.

Dissolve

Sleepy nausea, magic
                    leap that renders

dissolve, cross fade,
a bluff of logic.

Whereas the tree
                    retreats inside itself,
be it resolved. Just,
                    be it resolved. Film
for a few fudgy

seconds both
                is and *will be.*

And lurking
in the splice:
that the next picture
could be mud,
                    or psychedelic,

or less, some
                    half-charged battery

resigning, shutting
off the valves.

At its core — if it has

                        an exact midpoint —

like dusk, a day cross-

                        fading into night.

Whereas the tree

                        retreats inside itself,

be it resolved. Just,

                        be it resolved.

Webcam Screencap of Jonathan As Francis Bacon's *Self-Portrait, 1969*

When the world moves slower
than the mind. Faces
swirl, blurred not by the speed
of change but its opposite —
some material
sluggishness — the mind
a camera whipping around
the world, too fast to focus.

This is where I get confused.
How is he wildly identifiable,
helplessly himself even
in this smear, this pure
fist print of colour? Why
does that anger me, that
a part of a person is captured
by something so vague? Or,
I guess, I'm mad at another thing
he's showing us: *us*,
us as viewers — readers —
whizzing by, minds already wandering —

Glass Jaw

Under the floods, under a thu-thunking shoulder
check, I turn a mix of mean and happy,
chuck my helmet. Under my head flaps, cold
licks my locks, I grab great gobs

of jersey and wind up like the slinky arm
of a pinball machine. This is junior A,
so vicious. I will regret that I don't land
this punch — a wood finger finds the collapse

button behind my knees. There's speed,
then there's this: the clock stops.
On the ice, a braintube turns inside
out, I hear a zwupping pulse, like a sung

voice rewinding, It roars louder
than victory. Blade marks swoop
like screensaver lasers. I am seasick
on the liquids from my face.

All the light is out of order. Hey, buzzer!
I'm a sound wave, gamma rays,
steam, a swarm of fruit flies — inexact,
darting spots that bend magnification

out of 1:1. The rafters teach me —
I see the chilled air as it is: chemical, macho,

jelly. I am covered in it. It is thick
as olive oil. No. Caramel. No. Peanut butter.

Distortingly Proximal Pose

A Filofax of photos shot through a haze of bangs.
The Internet is a party where everyone except me

is sitting down, you're tempted to think, rifling
through blanched Gummi-bear portraits of your friends.

Credit the photo to an intimate twin of Andre the Giant.
But not. Like a resumé, self-snapped, arm at 90,

no, 120 degrees, a half heil, chin down, eyes up.
The extremities of one arm like a fish swimming

from the frame. You're dancing, waving, hailing a cab, leaning
on a wall for support. No, that arm is taking a self-portrait,

the sort of picture where self's italics. Look, she cranked
the saturation, her eyes like Ping-Pong balls. Look, here's

another distortingly proximal Myspace pose:
what lovely hardware he has in his eyebrow.

The practice of extending your lower lip without turning
your forehead to cornrows is as hard as you think.

On the chalkboard, a professor of media fills us in,
or just the moving parts: how did we get here? related

to spring-point snapshot buttons, lightweight
one-battery bodies, autofocus — only,

do they have chalkboards on Myspace?
Do they have teachers? Yeah, let's applaud

autofocus, essays due in two weeks on the nose. The subject
says *I took this photo two hundred times. I am now perfect.*

The photo says *Leave a comment. How do I format my comment?*
Post or preview comment.

If I Could See Ryan's Orgasm from the Inside, Then Technicolour

Telescoping, vision in pinhole, a twinkle, miles away,
    snowblindness, brink of blackout. Beacons, boys.
    Lighthouses and Sable Island.
Crumpling, newspaper pulled through a cardboard
    tube, elastic fabric cracking its tiny knuckles.
Tipping, sticky speed, weightless apex of swing, the
    stomach a bubble of tension, the gut a fermata.
    Pause absorbing a candied slacking.
Unclenching, a knot you can untie with your lips.
Stroke, stroke, hallucination, vivid underpinning,
    psychedelic extraworld to starve in.
Technicolour then, I'm guessing here, wires to uncross,
    eyes asleep, pins and needles, eyes astonished. The
    at-last, the lolling sprawl.
Noodle, will you walk again? What do your muscles
    say? Shh, oh, body bag of the senses,
lumberjack of pleasure, do away with courtesy. Mash up
    our manners. Spread them on our chests.

saxophones the lead parts.

8. There is no comparable way to
hold a human heart, although they both have
valves.

9. The saxophone was a pioneer of
French psychoanalytic theory, therefore *French*
is a misnomer, as in "French fries."

10. Playing the saxophone is a kind of
NPR, related through
    e counting side of the family.
G

News of the World

Riffles. Can't sit still.
Flaps, a curtain over a draft,
a kite in a field too small to catch.

Its cover a man who is unhappy
with his one wife, it floats

like a plastic wad,
trying to show you page three.
The story wants to *unfold*.

It in the subway newsstand
like an alto in an ASL choir,

a neighbour on a block
municipally reappraised,
a flashmobber taught

a simple dance.
Up, one, two, three. Down, one, two, three....

An ensign in an army of techies
tapping out telegraphs.
A tarp on a truck. Mudguards

in motion. Dreadlock
of party ribbon tied to a vent.

Point System

We are all the same is the moral of the story.
All men are the same is the moral of the story,
but it is not good news. Strangers should never
be encouraged is the moral of the story. Lose

and forfeit your job is the moral of the story.
Come off hard is the moral of the story.
The wolf lives and probably will get you
is the moral of the story. Resistance
is justified is the moral of the story.

Your "but Google is the moral of the story"
is the complete opposite of the truth. Think
before you act is the moral of the story. The last
line of the play is, "The moral of the story isn't
get along; it's get to know your neighbour."

Twenty-Two Ottawa Poets Fail to Agree about the Morning

A humble summoning of daylight.

Shower spray, sharp needles,
the speed limit, the streamlined
visible and beloved. When we were leaving
the sky-hole, this metal tent (plastic
on the grass, human beings
beaks aloft with ribbon)
blood, velocity and steam:

it falls the way a mind
becomes a corner
now cloud, fish, river, sea
cloud cloud cloud
of sad grey computer captains, the impedimenta
soft, on leather skin.

No stopping to browse The Terror Shop:
on Elgin Street, very little
of iron and carbon — these stories of metal
consigned pounds of paper to recycling. That too
is a bit much. We're related how?

Is this apocalypse parenthetical or parallel?
Be a saxophone disrupting sirens.
Hush baby, hush

Password Security Monologue

Should be kept as secret. Should not be shared
with anyone. Never tell anyone; you must not tell
it to anyone else. Never send it by email. Never tell
anyone over the telephone. Do not write it down.
Memorize it. Never write it on paper. Do not write it
on sticky notes, desk blotters or calendars.
If you must write it on a piece of paper, store the paper
in a secure place and destroy it when it is no longer needed.
Don't save it on your home personal computer.

The default for *remember password* should be *no*. If you log
on to your account using a computer that is not your home PC
and the computer asks you if you want to save it or remember it,
do not select *yes*. If you suspect that someone knows, change it.
If you think someone knows, change it immediately.

Password Security Drinking Game

Do not use your name or telephone number, names of family, pets, friends, co-workers or fantasy characters.

Do not use birthdays and other personal information.

Do not use your first, middle or last name, or anyone else's.

Do not use your initials or any nicknames for you or anyone else.

Do not use licence plate numbers, identification numbers, the brand of your automobile, the name of the street you live on or any hobbies.

Do not use your Social Security number or children's names.

Do not use dates, no matter the combination of words and numbers.

Do not use computer terms and names, commands, sites, companies, hardware or software.

Do not use slang, dialect or jargon.

Do not use common usage words.

Do not use any word from a dictionary.

Do not use a word contained in English or foreign
    dictionaries, spelling lists or other word lists and
    abbreviations.

Snake

Now. Now.

Now available
                on your mobile.

Aim at a food dot, grow.

Don't
swallow your tail. Now down. Now left.
Its lesson

is you're always moving
and can only decide which way.

Now your phone cries out
I'm tired, beep,
my batteries are almost
                        beep, beep,
having served two hours.

In a children's leaf pile,
slowly growing,
you heard your mom —

yes, even your mother —

say *now, now*.

Pissing on the Side of The Swarm, London, Ontario

It's not exactly privacy
so much as the illusion of privacy

that drives the stock of The Swarm
into the alley — summer night clouds,

the sky settling a score —
to let out acidically on the bricks.
One by one, smirking. Why this is
is partly the unencumbered pleasure

of a good piss. But also that your excess
will stir its vitamins into the earth.

Or, maybe, just having a public second
to yourself, yourself in your hands.

Under a Frypan-Pepsi-Burnt-out-House Sky

Trunk-packed family beater cradled
like a picnic, us sprinting through swatches
of night-knit panic. A radar in my child

self zinged. The K-car's fur pet me, my eyes
pitched over the door's plastic forearm,
reading a list of road. Tracheal tube

into a throat of forest, machine-assisted artery
to the rural, commuter, cottager — it nearly
orphaned me. In the nod of pine, a scudded

shuffle overhummed collisions vague but piling up.
It waits. Every stump, every boulder

a twitchy lurker under a frypan-Pepsi-
burnt-out-house sky. The forest's grin I dimly
understood but shrank from. A kidnapper's

pillowcase we booted through like we were chased
by dogs — every minute a roulette
of steel chambers. Click, nothing. Click, nothing.

This, from inside. From the shoulder,
we were smoke, a raft on rubber rapids,
a gated cage of tissue wind-wrapped, barely

a walk-on part, headlights and sedan's gawky
cough a hump rising, falling and blinking out.

An Ailment in the Major Constellations

Is this familiar? Being next to, near, but unable
finally to perch, the Legend of Symbols scrambled,
the Most Easily Decipherable Codex like a plaza
the point blows through, too high up to grab?
I mean, this is amateur hour. *This is*
amateur hour, right?

Our host intros the speaker like a Canadian
studies prof talking Scott —
needy, pompous, naïve —
and the room leans back, us the little dipper's
obtusest angle, the very shape
of a groan. We among ill pink plushes
of the Radisson Hotel and Suites Ballroom A

avert our eyes, the ghost
goes out of our faces. We do the cruellest
possible thing and let our minds wander.
At first, I think, we all want to be at least adjacent
to greatness. At least aware.
Then I think of a friend who lingers
on sad anecdotes — her own, especially —
how she really, deep down, is longing
to be the artist of mortality, to align
herself to an ailment in the major
constellations.
                    Then I think he wants

to be buried in greatness, or in all that effort
to have something great buried in him,
a tiny shard of the huge disco ball
of philosophy, or art, or — has he segued
to fly-fishing? — whatever. Noble, I guess.
But, *whoops*, he has us meditating
on a linear print of carpet, white china,
the pinprick in the waitress's face
where the piercing was till she started her shift.

Prayer II
Couplets to be read by two people at the same time

A scene in which we describe the difficulty of the project
    we first proposed.
A scene in which we describe the difficulty of the project
    we first proposed.

A scene in which we begin to depend on each other, and
    then retreat from it.
A scene in which we begin to depend on each other, and
    then regret it.

A scene in which menace is contemplated, then realized.
    Dark period. Grimace.
A scene in which menace is contemplated, then realized.
    Second act complications.

Traffic slides from a bolt like news awaiting embroidering.
Traffic rides in like bolt news, awaiting embroiling.

Long pauses in the conversation, while other stories persist
    silently or on cruise control.
Long pauses in the conversation, while other stories persist
    mumblingly or on cruise control.

Consolation was a great way to cap off the weekend.
Consternation was a grating way to cap off the weekend.

Nearly impregnable, brain looping an imaginary actual
    other encounter with the numerous.
Nearly impregnable, brain looping an imaginary actual
    other encounter with the numerous.

An understanding of "an understanding" that isn't snide
    or indulgent.
An understanding   that isn't snide
    or indulgent.

Us hardly one with the universe's Cosmic Reunion Tour,
    our jobs pulling at us like fingernails under wallpaper.
Us hardly one with the universe, imagining a reunion, our
    yob boyfriends at us, fingers in our underwear.

Us on our front stair, your head on my knees.
Us on our front stair, our head on our knees.

Us watching the street, its long shadows, it's nearly night.
Us watching the street, its   shadows, its nearly-night.

Yesterdayed.
Yesterdayed.

A kiss of electric fields, nearness, affinity, a gift to wait for.
A kiss of electric fields, filial, affinity, a gift to wait for.

Town in a Long Day of Leaving

Queen West, sternly placed, spread its mountain
of lingering arms to the favouring day.

Give to the Canadian the elastic, the uncommon —
the rich, mellow, thousand-brilliant, vivid dyes.

Sparkling, it had no other interest
than itself, to rivet, claim every thinking mind.

I heard many voices murmuring in the anxious
beings that thronged. Visibly, stupendous objects

ever flowed from human eyes. Rejoice for Canadian
and foreign united in friendship. St. Lawrence, King St...

to love Canada as I now love it — all comparisons
have wandered away. Then again,

the pleasure we experienced was not
a severe disappointment: amused at the extravagant,

entertained by the sight of the poorest and worst
dressed. Exhibited vanity, us, talked loudly of wealth,

brothers and sisters who had foolishly settled.
Beggarly, wooden country girls talked of the offer

of twelve dollars an hour. We tried with several
sober senses to inspect the land of absurd anticipations.

Both gentlemen and strangers, vulgar men gruffly
toward night, greatly dissatisfied, visit the city,

which they declare filthy. Two-hour summer town
in a long day of leaving, alarmed but not aware.

Here baffles us in the dark, the night a most stunning
confusion: my worst behaviour inspired me. Danger

is well preached to headstrong creatures. I dissolved
like wreaths of smoke. I a little jealous of Montreal, I

like the city. Listen to probabilities or be comforted.
All through the night, hear the oft-repeated name

of the sinking stricken city, gilding the mirrored sky,
billows of liquid the air seemed to light up.

Documents

The very caricature of the New Canadian
Novel, with its catty homage to anxiety, strain,
its epithets on office longing, Linda under a row of shotgun
keys runs her finger Z-X-C-V-B-N-

M, comma, period, slash/question mark. Sultry,
I guess, or else maddening. Tickety, tickety,
tickety. Linda: the kind of woman smart women
ruin the reputations of. She uses *like* to mean

both *as* and *as in*. We have a project,
and it isn't writing itself. If answers could be sucked
from the air through Linda's teeth, we'd have it sewn
up. They can't be. We are the moon rising in our own

office window. We're transfixed by the neon vest
of a construction worker idling by wet
concrete, concrete like a nerdy teen who, in the future,
will fall in with creatine and post bodybuilder

pictures of himself in a bikini on the internet, hoping
you'll see. And you do. As for the concrete, it's quivering.
We are hardly one with the Cosmic Reunion Tour,
our jobs pulling at us like fingernails under wallpaper.

The document miscarries, a half-formed
creature nobody loves. We leave it like a herd

of preschoolers abandoning craft supplies.
Either the office or I failed. Linda is not surprised.

•

The street squints. I linger in its lashes,
the setting concrete crusts. CAUTION brushes
over my head like something Greek; with idiot
ease I'm there, easing a finger in; idle thoughts —

of my skin like a tongue on winter
steel; of Gregory Peck at the Mouth of Truth — flicker.
It feels like slipping a digit
inside a frog. With all the snobbery of a poet

I pooh-pooh my own initials, trace an *a*, lower
case — a circle with descender
rather than an *a* waving its mutant extra
arm. I surprise myself, just *a*,

in the texture of scud. I think writing was gooey
before touch-typing, then my mind coolly
adds, "*old school*," like an ageing man-boy
investigating slang. Don't worry,

I laughed at me too. Crouching beside the *a*, my mind's
beach bum brother slinking off to flirt with words
too long for concrete, my finger slickly
adds a second *a* — *aa* it says, as if to spite me,

its spitefulness being, I admit, my own. Then,
with my mind more at the levers than
before, I add two *b*s — *aabb* — and stand,
wet finger in my pocket, hoping it doesn't bond.

Acknowledgements

Earlier drafts of these poems have appeared in *CV2*, *ditch,,*, *Dusty Owl Quarterly*, *The Fiddlehead*, *The Malahat Review*, *The Moose and Pussy*, *Ottawater* and the *Peter F. Yacht Club*; the anthologies *Pent Up* (Angel House Press, 2009) and *Rogue Stimulus* (Mansfield Press, 2010); and the chapbooks *Heteroskeptical*, *Town in a Long Day of Leaving* and *The Glass Jaw*.

Notes

This manuscript contains the entire text of Don McKay's "Some Functions of a Leaf" (*Camber*, McClelland & Stewart, 2004) spread over seventeen poems. "Song for the Song of Britney Spears" owes some of its cyborginess to Genevieve Koski's Onion (A.V. Club) review of Spears' *Femme Fatale* (March 29, 2011). The italicized lines in "Earthenware Mug" are from Tim Lilburn's "Kill-site" (*Kill-site*, McClelland & Stewart, 2003). The epigraph at the beginning of the book is from David W. McFadden's *Gypsy Guitar* (Talon, 1987). "Point System" and the two password poems both use found text from the Internet, some of it treated, most of it in its original form. "Town in a Long Day of Leaving" plunders a chapter from Suzanna Moodie's *Roughing It in the Bush* (1852). Section 91(9) of the *Constitution Act 1867 (The BNA Act)* is lodged in "If I Could See Ryan's Orgasm from the Inside, Then Technicolour."

The lines of "Twenty-Two Toronto Poets Wake Up on the Bathroom Floor and Discuss Their Hangover" are from, in order of appearance, Nick Thran ("Aria with a Mirror and No Earplugs," *The Best Canadian Poetry in English 2010*, Tightrope Books, 2010); Michael Redhill ("Getting sick," *Impromptu Feats of Balance*, Wolsak and Wynn, 1990); Dennis Lee ("Thursday," *Civil Elegies*, House of Anansi, 1972); Michael Ondaatje ("The Siyabaslakara," *Handwriting*, McClelland & Stewart,

1998); Adam Sol ("Right Lane Must Exit," *Jeremiah, Ohio*, House of Anansi, 2008); Don Coles ("Three Tolstoy Poems," *The Prinzhorn Collection*, Macmillan of Canada, 1982); Suzanne Buffam ("The Arena," *The Irrationalist*, House of Anansi, 2010); Milton Acorn ("The completion on the fiddle," *Captain Neal MacDougal and the Naked Goddess*, Ragweed, 1982); Ken Babstock ("Palindromic" *Airstream Land Yacht*, House of Anansi, 2006); Stephen Cain ["1994: Naked (Mike Leigh): 126 min.," *Torontology*, ECW, 2001]; Margaret Christakos ("Offshore 3," *wipe.under.a.love*, Mansfield, 2000); Lynn Crosbie ["Scream in High Park (July 19, 1993)," *Alphabet City*, House of Anansi, 1998]; Margaret Avison ("New Year's Poem," *15 Canadian Poets Plus 5*, Gary Geddes, ed., Oxford UP, 1978); Matt Tierney ("Pallbearers," *Full Speed through the Morning Dark*, Wolsak and Wynn, 2004); Karen Solie ("Prayers for the Sick," *Pigeon*, House of Anansi, 2010); Ryan Kamstra ("tHe wEST, kICKER," *Into the Drowned World*, Insomniac, 2008); Sandra Alland ("Seilful Tids/Seizure Tides," *Blissful Times*, BookThug, 2007); Ron Charach ("Squeezing the Barbarians," *Dungenessque*, Signature, 2001); Sky Gilbert ("He Should Be As a Bar or Tavern Is," *Temptations for a Juvenile Delinquent*, ECW, 2003); Stuart Ross ("The Boys," Proper Tales Press broadsheet, 2007); Rachel Zolf ("22.12," *Neighbour Procedure*, Coach House, 2010); and Helen Guri ("Resonance Is a Direction," *Match*, Coach House, 2011), respectively.

The lines of "Twenty-Two BC Poets Use Orgasm As

a Metaphor for Belonging" are from, in order of appearance, Meredith Quartermain ("Frost," *Recipes from the Red Planet*, BookThug, 2010); Billeh Nickerson ("It's Hard to Say No," *The Asthmatic Glassblower*, Arsenal Pulp, 2000); Peter Culley ("A Book of Quiet Numbers," *Hammertown*, New Star, 2003); Sonnet L'Abbé ("The Trees Have Loved Us All Along," *The Best Canadian Poetry in English 2010*, Tightrope, 2010); Brenda Leifso ("What do you want?" *In Fine Form*, Kate Braid and Sandy Shreve, eds., Raincoast, 2005); Gil McElroy ("Missionary Machines," *Last Scattering Surfaces*, Talon, 2007); Earle Birney ("A Walk in Kyoto," *15 Canadian Poets Plus 5*, Gary Geddes, ed., Oxford UP, 1978); Eric Miller ("The Question," *In the Scaffolding*, Goose Lane, 2005); Esta Spalding ("Train Window," *The Wife's Account*, House of Anansi, 2002); Sean Horlor ("For St. Fiacre," *Seminal*, Arsenal Pulp, 2007); Michael V. Smith ("Salvation," *Seminal*, Arsenal Pulp, 2007); George Bowering ("Desert Elm iv," *The Catch*, McClelland & Stewart, 1976); Anna Swanson ("Medusa's lullaby," *The Nights Also*, Tightrope, 2010); Elizabeth Bachinsky ("At Roberts Creek," *God of Missed Connections*, Nightwood, 2009); Tim Bowling ("The Return," *The Book Collector*, Nightwood, 2008); A.F. Moritz ("Philosophical Content," *The Sentinel*, House of Anansi, 2008); George McWhirter ("An Era of Easu Meat at Locarno," *The Incorrections*, Oolichan, 2007); Alice Major ("Give the city its three names," *The Occupied World*, U of Alberta P, 2006); Tom Wayman ("Teaching English," *The Best*

Canadian Poetry in English 2009, Tightrope, 2009);
Sharon Thesen ("The Parrot," *News & Smoke*, Talon,
1999); Pat Lowther ("Notes From Furry Creek," *15
Canadian Poets Plus 5*, Gary Geddes, ed., Oxford UP,
1978); and Matt Rader ("The Weather Makers," *Living
Things*, Nightwood, 2008), respectively.

The lines of "Twenty-Two Ottawa Poets Fail to Agree
about the Morning" are from, in order of appearance,
Sandra Ridley ("Lift: Ghazals for C," *Fallout*, Hagios,
2010); Anita Dolman ("Blame," *Scalpel, tea and shot glass*,
above/ground, 2004); John Barton ("Confidential," *Sweet
Ellipsis*, ECW, 1998); Diana Brebner ("The Blue Light
of the Neutron Pool," *The Ishtar Gate*, McGill-Queen's
UP, 2005); Anita Lahey ("Travel Photos," *The New
Canon*, Signal, 2005); Joe Hickey ("Once He Was a
Dinosaur," *Dinosaur Porn*, Ferno & TERU, 2010);
Gwendolyn Guth ("Good People," *Purdyesque*,
above/ground, 2006); Leigh Nash ("Towards the Last
Spike," *five-seven-five: train poems*, TERU, 2008); Shane
Rhodes ("Entanglements," *The Bindery*, NeWest, 2007);
Cameron Anstee ("Other Surfaces," *Remembering Our
Young Bones*, In/Words, 2008); Stephen Brockwell
("Compulsive in the Public Library," *Cometology*, ECW,
2001); Pearl Pirie ("all the time i wanted to," *been shed
bore*, Chaudiere, 2010); John Newlove ("It's Winter in
Ottawa," *The Tasmanian Devil*, above/ground, 1999);
Roland Prevost ("Post Hoc Sleepwalk," *Our/Are Carried
Invisibles*, above/ground, 2009); Nicholas Lea ("Dear
You," *Everything Is Movies*, Chaudiere, 2007); rob

mclennan ("fourteen hearts; a grist," *a compact of words*, Salmon, 2009); David O'Meara ("Structural Steel," *The Vicinity*, Brick, 2003); Anne Le Dressay ("Letter looking forward," *Old Winter*, Chaudiere, 2007); Andrew Faulkner ("Proposition," *Useful knots and how to tie them*, TERU, 2008); Amanda Earl ("Eve in the Garden of Armageddon," AngelHousePress, undated); George Elliott Clarke ("Poetry: 1/7/75–1/7/05" *Black*, Polestar, 2006); Jacqueline Lawrence ("Surrender ix," *Surrender*, In/Words, undated), respectively.